Digital Dollars

Unveiling the Secrets to Generating Multiple Online Income Streams

Henry S. Norman

TABLE OF CONTENTS

Introduction

Welcome to Digital Dollars: Unveiling the Secrets to Generating Multiple Online Income Streams. This book is your ultimate guide to making money online in the digital age. Whether you are looking for a side hustle, a full-time income, or a passive income, this book will show you the different ways you can earn money online, and how to choose, start, and grow your online income stream.

Why Make Money Online?

Making money online is not only a convenient and flexible way to earn income but also a smart and strategic way to leverage the power of the internet. By making money online, you can:

• Access a global market of customers and clients who are eager to pay for your products, services, or content

• Create multiple streams of income that can generate passive income for you, even when you are sleeping

• Reduce your expenses and overhead costs by working from anywhere, anytime, and with minimal equipment

• Learn new skills and gain valuable experience in the digital economy, which is constantly evolving and growing.

• Reach for the stars and accomplish your personal and professional goals, whether it is to boost your income, leave your job, or achieve financial freedom.

The internet has opened up a world of possibilities and opportunities for you to make money online. You can sell products, sell services, create content, teach online, or invest online.

You can use your existing skills, knowledge, or passions, or learn new ones. You can choose your own work environment, schedule, and pace. You can achieve financial freedom and flexibility, and live the lifestyle you want.

But making money online is not a walk in the park. It requires hard work, dedication, and persistence. It also requires knowledge, skills, and strategies. It also requires trial and error, learning from mistakes, and adapting to changes.

This book is designed to help you achieve your online income goals and dreams. This book will provide you with the comprehensive and practical information you need to succeed in your online income journey.

In this book, you will learn:

• The benefits and challenges of each online income stream

• The best practices and tips to succeed in each online income stream

• The steps and actions you need to take to start and grow your online income stream

• The tools and resources you need to support your online income stream

• The mindset and habits you need to develop to make money online.

By the end of this book, you will have a clear idea of what online income stream suits you best, and how to get started and grow your online income.

You will also have a realistic and practical mindset that will help you overcome any obstacles and challenges that you may face along the way.

You will also have a vision and a plan that will guide you toward your online income goals and dreams.

This book is not the end of your online income journey. It is only the beginning. There is so much more to learn and discover in the online world.

Some new trends and opportunities emerge every day. There are new skills and strategies that you can acquire and improve.

I also encourage you to share and teach others what you have learned and experienced in your online income journey.

I hope you are excited and ready to start your online income journey. Thank you for choosing this book and trusting me with your online income education. I wish you all the best and success in your online income endeavors.

Remember, the online world is full of possibilities and potential. You have to make a move and realize your dreams. Now, let's dive into the first chapter and learn about diverse online income streams.

Chapter 1

What are Online Income Streams?

You have a dream, a passion, and a skill. You want to make money online and enjoy the freedom and flexibility of your online lifestyle. But how do you do that? How do you turn your dream, passion, and skill into a profitable and sustainable online business? The answer is simple: you create online income streams.

Online income streams are ways of earning money from the internet, without having to work actively for every dollar. Online income streams can be passive, meaning they require little or no maintenance, or active, meaning they require some work or involvement from the creator. Some examples of online income streams are:

• Selling products or services online, such as through e-commerce, dropshipping, print-on-demand, or freelancing

• Creating content online, such as through blogging, podcasting, video making, or online courses

• Monetizing your content online, such as through advertising, sponsorships, subscriptions, or donations

• Investing online, such as through stocks, real estate, or cryptocurrencies

• Using passive income apps, such as cashback, survey, or reward apps

Online income streams can be a great way to diversify your income, achieve financial freedom, and leverage the power of the internet. However, they also come with some challenges, such as competition, saturation, scams, and technical issues.

Therefore, it is important to do your research, choose the best online income stream for you, and follow the best practices to succeed online.

Categories of Online Income Streams and how they function

• **Selling products or services:** This is where you create or offer a product or service that solves a problem or meets a need for your target audience, and sell it online. You can sell physical products, such as clothing, books, or gadgets, or digital products, such as ebooks, courses, or software. You can also sell services, such as web design, consulting, or coaching. You can sell your products or services on your website, blog, store, or platforms like Amazon, Etsy, or Fiverr. You can earn money from each sale or transaction that you make online.

• **Creating content:** This is where you produce and distribute valuable and engaging content, such as articles, videos, podcasts, or ebooks, to a target audience online. You can create content on various topics, such as entertainment, education, lifestyle, gaming, or business.

You can create and monetize your content on your website, blog, channel, or platforms like [YouTube], [Medium], or [Spotify]. You can earn money from various sources, such as advertising, sponsorship, subscription, or donation.

• **Advertising:** This is where you display or promote ads on your website, blog, or channel, or on platforms like [Google Ads], [Facebook Ads], or [Instagram Ads]. You can display or promote ads from other businesses or brands that are relevant to your niche or audience. You can earn money from the number of views, clicks, or conversions that the ads generate.

• **Affiliate marketing:** This is where you share or promote products or services from other businesses or brands that are relevant to your niche or audience, and earn a commission for each sale or action that you inspire.

You can use platforms like Amazon Associates, ShareASale, or ClickBank to find and join affiliate programs that suit your niche or audience. You can use links, banners, or widgets to showcase the affiliate products or services on your website, blog, or channel.

• **Freelancing:** This is where you showcase your skills or services to clients online, usually on a project-by-project or contract basis.

You can offer skills or services such as writing, editing, graphic design, programming, or translation.

You can use platforms like [Upwork], [Freelancer], or [Guru] to find and apply for freelance projects that suit your skills or services. You can earn money from the fees or rates that you deserve for your work.

• **Consulting:** This is where you provide expert advice or guidance to clients online, usually on a one-on-one or group basis. You can provide advice or guidance on topics such as business, marketing, finance, or health.

You can use platforms like [Clarity], and [Coach. me], or [Savvy] to find and connect with clients who need your expertise. You can earn money from the fees or rates that you value for your consultation.

• **Teaching:** This is where you teach or tutor students online, usually on a one-on-one or group basis. You can teach or tutor subjects such as languages, math, science, or music.

You can use platforms like [Udemy], [Skillshare], or [Wyzant] to create and sell your courses or lessons, or to find and connect with students who need your instruction. You can earn money from the fees or rates that you charge for your teaching or tutoring.

These are some of the common types and categories of online income streams and how they work. Of course, there are many more ways to make money online, and the possibilities are endless.

The key is to find something that suits your skills, interests, and goals, and to keep learning, experimenting, and adapting to the changing online landscape.

The benefits and challenges of online income streams Online income streams can offer many benefits and challenges for anyone who wants to make money online.

Benefits of Online Income Streams

• **Flexibility and freedom:** Online income streams can give you more flexibility and freedom over your work schedule, location, and lifestyle.

You can work when, where, and how you want, without being tied to a fixed office or employer. You can also pursue your passions, hobbies, or interests, and create a work-life balance that suits you.

• **Scalability and diversity:** Online income streams can allow you to scale and diversify your income potential, by creating multiple sources of revenue that are not dependent on your time or effort.

You can leverage the power of automation, outsourcing, or passive income to increase your earnings, reduce your risk, and explore new opportunities for your online business.

• **Creativity and innovation:** Online income streams can enable you to express your creativity and innovation, by producing and delivering valuable and engaging content, products, or services to your target audience. You can also use the latest technology, tools, and trends to enhance your online presence, brand, and authority, and stand out from the competition.

Challenges of Online Income Streams

• **Knowledge and skills:** Online income streams require you to have the relevant knowledge and skills to provide value to your customers or clients. You need to learn and master the technical, business, and marketing aspects of your online income stream, and keep up with the changing online landscape.

You also need to invest in your education and development and learn from experts, courses, books, blogs, podcasts, etc.

• **Patience and persistence:** Online income streams are not get-rich-quick schemes. They require time, effort, and dedication to grow and generate income. You need to set realistic goals and expectations, track your progress and results, celebrate your wins, and learn from your failures.

You also need to find a mentor, a coach, or a community to support you and keep you motivated.

• **Preparedness and flexibility:** Online income streams are constantly evolving and changing due to market trends, customer preferences, technology updates, and competition.

You need to be prepared and flexible to adapt to the changes and opportunities. You need to research your niche and audience, test your ideas and products, collect feedback and data, and improve your offers and strategies.

How to Choose the Best Online Income Stream

Choosing the best online income stream for you depends on several factors, such as your skills, interests, goals, budget, and time. Here are some steps you can take to choose the best online income stream for you:

Assess your skills and interests: The first step is to assess your skills and interests and identify what you are good at, what you enjoy doing, and what you want to learn or improve.

You can use tools like [Skillshare] or [Udemy] to explore and learn new skills or take online tests like [16Personalities] or [Myers-Briggs] to discover more about yourself and your personality type.

You can also look at your hobbies, passions, or problems, and see if you can turn them into online income opportunities.

Research the market and the demand: The second step is to research the market and the demand and find out what problems or needs your target audience has, and how you can solve them or meet them with your online income offer.

You can use tools like [Google Trends], [Amazon Best Sellers], or [BuzzSumo] to find and analyze current trends, popular products, and viral content in your niche or industry.

You can also use platforms like [Quora], [Reddit], or [Facebook Groups] to interact with your potential customers or clients and get insights into their pain points, preferences, and feedback.

Evaluate the competition and the differentiation: The third step is to evaluate the competition and the differentiation and see what solutions or alternatives already exist in the market, and how you can differentiate yourself from them.

You can use tools like [SEMrush], [Ahrefs], or [SimilarWeb] to spy on your competitors and see their traffic, keywords, backlinks, and content strategies. You can also use platforms like [Trustpilot], [Yelp], or [Amazon Reviews] to read the reviews and ratings of your competitors, and see their strengths, weaknesses, and areas of improvement.

You can then use your unique selling proposition (USP), which is the main benefit or value that you offer to your customers or clients, to stand out from the crowd and attract more attention and sales.

Test your idea and your product: The fourth step is to test your idea and your product and see if it is viable, feasible, and desirable in the market.

You can use tools like [Google Forms], [SurveyMonkey], or [Typeform] to create and distribute surveys or polls to your target audience and get their opinions, feedback, and suggestions.

You can also use platforms like [Kickstarter], [Indiegogo], or [Patreon] to launch and fund your idea or product, and see if there is enough interest and support from your potential customers or clients.

You can then use the data and feedback you collect to validate and improve your idea or product and make it more appealing and profitable.

Launch and market your online income stream: The fifth step is to launch and market your online income stream and start generating income from your online business. You can use platforms like [WordPress], [Shopify], [YouTube], [Udemy], etc. to create and host your online income platform, such as a website, blog, store, channel, or course.

You can also use channels and strategies like social media, email, content, ads, campaigns, collaborations, etc. to promote and market your online income offer and build trust and relationships with your audience.

You can also use analytics and tools like [Google Analytics], [Facebook Pixel], or [Mailchimp] to track and measure your performance and results and optimize and improve your online income stream.

These are some of the steps you can take to choose the best online income stream for you.

Of course, there are many more details and nuances involved in each step, and you will need to learn, experiment, and adapt to the changing online landscape. But the most important thing is to take action and persist in your online income journey.

Chapter 2

Selling Products Online

In this chapter, you will discover how to make money online by selling products. Selling products online is one of the most exciting and rewarding online income streams. You can sell physical products, such as clothes, books, or gadgets, or digital products, such as ebooks, courses, or software.

You can create your products, source them from suppliers, or use print-on-demand services. You can sell your products on your website, on e-commerce platforms, or social media.

The Benefits of Selling Products Online

- You can reach a large global market of eager customers

- You can build your brand and reputation

- You can set your prices and profit margins

- You can automate and scale your online store

- You can express your creativity and passion

The Challenges of Selling Products Online

- You have to overcome competition and saturation

- You have to handle inventory, shipping, and customer service

- You have to comply with legal and tax regulations

- You have to invest time and money upfront

- You have to market and promote your products effectively

How to Succeed in Selling Products Online

In order to succeed in selling your products on online you will need to:

- Choose the right products to sell

- Choose the right platform to sell your products

- Choose the right pricing and payment methods

- Choose the right marketing and promotion strategies

- Choose the right tools and resources to support your online store

In the following sections, we will explore each of these steps in more detail.

Section 1: Choosing the Right Products to Sell

The first step in selling products online is to choose the right products to sell. The right products are the ones that:

- Solve a problem or fulfill a need for your target market

- Have a high demand and low supply

- Have a unique selling proposition or competitive advantage

- Have a reasonable size and weight

- A long shelf life and low maintenance

To choose the right products to sell, you can:

- Do market research and find out what your potential customers want and need

- Do competitor analysis and find out what your competitors are selling and how they are selling it

- Do product validation and test your product idea with your potential customers

- Do product sourcing and find the best suppliers or manufacturers for your products

Section 2: Choosing the Right Platform to sell your products

The second step in selling products online is to choose the right platform to sell your products. The right platform is the one that:

- Matches your product type and niche

- Has a large and relevant audience

- Has a user-friendly and secure interface

- Has a low cost and high commission

- A good reputation and customer service

- Has good integration and customization options

To choose the right platform to sell your products, you can:

- Compare the pros and cons of different platforms, such as your website, e-commerce platforms, or social media

- Consider the features and functionalities of different platforms, such as inventory management, payment processing, shipping options, analytics, etc.

- Consider the policies and regulations of different platforms, such as fees, taxes, refunds, disputes, etc.

- Consider the feedback and reviews of different platforms, such as customer satisfaction, seller support, etc.

- Consider the compatibility and flexibility of different platforms, such as design, branding, SEO, etc.

Section 3: Choosing the Right Pricing and Payment Methods

The third step in selling products online is to choose the right pricing and payment methods. The right pricing and payment methods are the ones that:

- Reflect on the value and quality of your products

- Attract and retain your customers

- Cover your costs and expenses

- Generate your desired profit

- Comply with legal and tax requirements

- Ensure security and convenience

To choose the right pricing and payment methods, you can:

- Do competitor analysis and find out what your competitors are charging and offering

- Do a cost analysis and find out your fixed and variable costs, such as production, shipping, platform fees, etc.

- Do a profit analysis and find out your break-even point, profit margin, and revenue goals

- Do pricing strategies and find out the best pricing model, such as cost-plus, value-based, dynamic, etc.

- Do payment options and find out the best payment methods, such as credit cards, PayPal, Stripe, etc.

- Do payment security and find out the best payment gateways, such as SSL, PCI, etc.

Section 4: Choosing the Right Marketing and Promotion Strategies

The fourth step in selling products online is to choose the right marketing and promotion strategies. The right marketing and promotion strategies are the ones that:

- Increase your brand awareness and visibility

- Increase your traffic and conversions

- Increase your customer loyalty and retention

- Increase your referrals and word-of-mouth

- Increase your sales and revenue

To choose the right marketing and promotion strategies, you can:

- Do market segmentation and find out your target market and audience, such as demographics, psychographics, behavior, etc.

- Do market positioning and find out your unique selling proposition and competitive advantage, such as benefits, features, values, etc.

- Do marketing mix and find out the best combination of product, price, place, and promotion, such as quality, value, distribution, and communication

- Do marketing channels and find out the best platforms and mediums to reach your audience, such as website, email, social media, etc.

- Do marketing tactics and find out the best methods and techniques to engage your audience, such as content, SEO, ads, etc.

- Do marketing metrics and find out the best ways to measure and improve your marketing performance, such as traffic, conversions, retention, etc.

Section 5: Choosing the Right Tools and Resources to Support your Online Store

The fifth and final step in selling products online is to choose the right tools and resources to support your online store. The right tools and resources are the ones that:

- Enhance and optimize your online store performance

- Save and reduce your online store costs

- Learn and improve your online store skills

- Grow and scale your online store business

To choose the right tools and resources to support your online store, you can:

- Compare the features and functionalities of different tools and resources, such as inventory management, shipping, analytics, etc.

- Consider the costs and benefits of different tools and resources, such as fees, commissions, discounts, etc.

- Consider the feedback and reviews of different tools and resources, such as customer satisfaction, seller support, etc.

- Consider the compatibility and flexibility of different tools and resources, such as integration, customization, etc.

- Consider the learning and improvement opportunities of different tools and resources, such as tutorials, courses, blogs, etc.

Summary

In this chapter, you discover how to make money online by selling products. You explored how to choose the right products, platform, pricing, marketing, and tools for your online store. You also uncovered the benefits and challenges of selling products online and the best practices and tips to thrive in this online income stream.

Chapter 3

Selling Services Online

In this chapter, you will discover how to make money online by selling services. Selling services online is another exciting and rewarding online income stream. You can sell your skills, knowledge, or expertise to people who need them.

You can offer services such as consulting, coaching, writing, designing, programming, or anything else that you can do remotely. You can create your services, join a platform, or work as a freelancer. You can sell your services on your website, on service marketplaces, or social media.

Benefits of selling services online

- You can leverage your existing skills and experience

- You can set your rates and terms

- You can work from anywhere and anytime

- You can build your reputation and credibility

- You can establish long-term relationships with your clients

The challenges of Selling Services Online

- You have to overcome competition and saturation

- You have to deliver high-quality work and meet deadlines

- You have to deal with communication and collaboration issues

- You have to manage your time and workload

- You have to market and promote your services effectively

How to Succeed in Selling Services Online

To succeed in selling services online, you need to:

- Choose the right services to sell

- Choose the right platform to sell your services

- Choose the right pricing and payment methods

- Choose the right marketing and promotion strategies

- Choose the right tools and resources to support your service business

In the sections that follow, we will dive deeper into each of these steps.

Section 1: Choosing the Right Services to Sell

The first step in selling services online is to choose the right services to sell.

The services you want are those that:

- Match your skills, interests, and passions

- Solve a problem or fulfill a need for your target market

- Have a high demand and low supply

- Have a clear scope and deliverables

- Have a measurable outcome and value

To choose the right services to sell, you can:

- Do a self-assessment and find out your strengths and weaknesses, what you love doing, and what you are good at

- Do market research and find out what your potential clients want and need, and what they are willing and able to pay

- Do competitor analysis and find out what your competitors are offering and how they are offering it

- Do service validation and test your service idea with your potential clients

- Do service creation and define your service offering, such as the name, description, benefits, features, etc.

Section 2: Choosing the Right Platform to Sell your Services

The second step in selling services online is to choose the right platform to sell your services.

- The best platform for you is the one that:

- Matches your service type and niche

- Has a large and relevant audience

- Has a user-friendly and secure interface

- Has a low cost and high commission

- Has a good reputation and customer service

- Has good integration and customization options

To choose the right platform to sell your services, you can:

- Compare the pros and cons of different platforms, such as your website, service marketplaces, or social media

- Consider the features and functionalities of different platforms, such as booking, invoicing, messaging, reviews, etc.

- Consider the policies and regulations of different platforms, such as fees, taxes, refunds, disputes, etc.

- Consider the feedback and reviews of different platforms, such as customer satisfaction, seller support, etc.

- Consider the compatibility and flexibility of different platforms, such as design, branding, SEO, etc.

Some examples of platforms where you can sell your services online are:

-**Fiverr** is a platform where you can sell any kind of service, starting from $5. You can create your gigs, or browse through the categories and subcategories to find the best fit for your service.

-**Upwork** is a platform where you can sell professional services, such as writing, designing, programming, etc. You can create your profile, or bid on projects posted by clients.

-**Clarity** is a platform where you can sell business advice, coaching, or consulting. You can create your profile, set your hourly rate, and take calls from clients who need your expertise.

-**Skillshare** is a platform where you can sell online courses, workshops, or tutorials. You can create your classes, or join the teacher community and get access to resources and support.

-**Coaching** is a platform where you can sell coaching services, such as life coaching, career coaching, health coaching, etc. You can create your profile, set your prices, and schedule sessions with clients.

Section 3: Choosing the Right Pricing and Payment Methods

The third step in selling services online is to choose the right pricing and payment methods.

The right pricing and payment methods are the ones that:

- Reflect on the value and quality of your services

- Attract and retain your clients

- Cover your costs and expenses

- Generate your desired profit

- Comply with legal and tax requirements

- Ensure security and convenience

To choose the right pricing and payment methods, you can:

- Do market research and find out what your clients are willing and able to pay

- Do competitor analysis and find out what your competitors are charging and offering

- Do a cost analysis and find out your fixed and variable costs, such as platform fees, tools, taxes, etc.

- Do a profit analysis and find out your break-even point, profit margin, and revenue goals

- Do pricing strategies and find out the best pricing model, such as hourly, fixed, value-based, etc.

- Do payment options and find out the best payment methods, such as credit cards, PayPal, Stripe, etc.

- Do payment security and find out the best payment gateways, such as SSL, PCI, etc.

Section 4: Choosing the Right Marketing and Promotion Strategies

The fourth step in selling services online is to choose the right marketing and promotion strategies. The right marketing and promotion strategies are the ones that:

- Increase your brand awareness and visibility

- Increase your traffic and conversions

- Increase your customer loyalty and retention

- Increase your referrals and word-of-mouth

- Increase your sales and revenue

To choose the right marketing and promotion strategies, you can:

- Do market segmentation and find out your target market and audience, such as demographics, psychographics, behavior, etc.

- Do market positioning and find out your unique selling proposition and competitive advantage, such as benefits, features, values, etc.

- Do marketing mix and find out the best combination of product, price, place, and promotion, such as quality, value, distribution, and communication

- Do marketing channels and find out the best platforms and mediums to reach your audience, such as website, email, social media, etc.

- Do marketing tactics and find out the best methods and techniques to engage your audience, such as content, SEO, ads, etc.

- Do marketing metrics and find out the best ways to measure and improve your marketing performance, such as traffic, conversions, retention, etc.

Section 5: Choosing the Right Tools and Resources to Support your Service Business

The fifth and final step in selling services online is to choose the right tools and resources to support your service business. The right tools and resources are the ones that:

- Simplify and automate your service business operations

- Enhance and optimize your service business performance

- Save and reduce your service business costs

- Learn and improve your service business skills

- Grow and scale your service business

To choose the right tools and resources to support your service business, you can:

- Compare the features and functionalities of different tools and resources, such as booking, invoicing, messaging, reviews, etc.

- Consider the costs and benefits of different tools and resources, such as fees, commissions, discounts, etc.

- Consider the feedback and reviews of different tools and resources, such as customer satisfaction, seller support, etc.

- Consider the compatibility and flexibility of different tools and resources, such as integration, customization, etc.

- Consider the learning and improvement opportunities of different tools and resources, such as tutorials, courses, blogs, etc.

Some examples of tools and resources that can help you sell your services online are:

Calendly is a tool that helps you schedule appointments and meetings with your clients. You can set your availability, share your link, and let your clients book a time slot with you.

FreshBooks is a tool that helps you create and send invoices, track payments, and manage your accounting. You can also accept online payments, send reminders, and generate reports.

Zoom is a tool that helps you conduct video calls, webinars, and online meetings with your clients. You can also share your screen, record your sessions, and chat with your participants.

Mailchimp is a tool that helps you create and send email campaigns, newsletters, and automation to your clients. You can also segment your audience, personalize your messages, and track your results.

Canva is a tool that helps you create and design graphics, logos, flyers, and social media posts for your service business. You can also use templates, icons, fonts, and images.

Summary

In this chapter, you discover how to make money online by selling services. You explored how to choose the right services, platform, pricing, marketing, and tools for your service business. You also uncovered the benefits and challenges of selling services online and the best practices and tips to thrive in this online income stream.

In the next chapter, you will unlock the secrets of making money online by creating content. You will find out how to choose the right content type, niche, format, and style for your audience.

You will also reveal the benefits and challenges of creating content online and the best practices and tips to excel in this online income stream.

You will dive into the different types of content you can create, such as blogs, podcasts, videos, ebooks, courses, etc. You will also discover the different platforms and channels you can use to distribute and monetize your content, such as websites, social media, email, etc.

You will learn how to create engaging and valuable content that attracts and retains your audience, and how to optimize and promote your content to increase your traffic and conversions. You will also learn how to use analytics and tools to measure and improve your content performance and results.

Chapter 4

Creating Content Online

In this chapter, you will discover how to make money online by creating content. Creating content online is another exciting and rewarding online income stream. You can create content such as blog posts, videos, podcasts, ebooks, courses, or anything else that provides value to your audience. You can create content on your website, on content platforms, or social media.

The Benefits of Creating Content Online

-You can showcase your expertise and authority

-You can attract and engage your target audience

-You can monetize your content in various ways

-You can build your brand and reputation

-You can express your creativity and passion

The Challenges of Creating Content Online

-You have to produce high-quality and original content

-You have to research and optimize your content for search engines and users

-You have to publish and update your content regularly

-You have to overcome competition and saturation

-You have to market and promote your content effectively

How to Succeed in Creating Content Online

To succeed in creating content online, you need to:

- Choose the right content to create

- Choose the right platform to create your content

- Choose the right monetization methods for your content

- Choose the right marketing and promotion strategies for your content

- Choose the right tools and resources to support your content creation

We will go into more detail about each of these steps in the following sections

Section 1: Choosing the Right Content to Create

The first step in creating content online is to choose the right content to create. You should create content that:

- Matches your skills, interests, and passions

- Solves a problem or fulfills a need for your target audience.

We will go into more detail about each of these steps in the following sections

- Has a high demand and low supply

- Has a unique angle or perspective

- Has a clear purpose and value

To choose the right content to create, you can:

- Do a self-assessment and find out your strengths and weaknesses, what you love doing, and what you are good at

- Do market research and find out what your potential audience wants and needs, and what they are searching for online

- Do competitor analysis and find out what your competitors are creating and how they are creating it

- Do content validation and test your content idea with your potential audience

- Do content planning and outline your content structure, format, and style

Some examples of content types that you can create online are:

Blog posts are written articles that provide information, insights, opinions, or stories on a specific topic. Blog posts can help you rank for keywords, drive traffic, and generate leads. You can create blog posts on your website, or platforms like Medium or WordPress.

Videos are visual and audio content that provide entertainment, education, or inspiration on a specific topic. Videos can help you reach a large and engaged audience, build trust, and increase conversions. You can create videos on your website, or platforms like YouTube or [TikTok].

Podcasts are audio content that provides conversations, interviews, or stories on a specific topic. Podcasts can help you grow your audience, establish your authority, and create loyal fans. You can create podcasts on your website or platforms like [Spotify] or [Anchor].

Ebooks are digital books that provide in-depth knowledge, guidance, or advice on a specific topic. Ebooks can help you generate revenue, capture leads, and showcase your expertise. You can create ebooks on your website, or platforms like [Amazon Kindle] or [Gumroad].

Courses are online learning programs that provide instruction, feedback, or certification on a specific topic. Courses can help you generate revenue, build your brand, and share your skills. You can create courses on your website or platforms like [Udemy] or [Skillshare].

Section 2: Choosing the Right Platform to Create your Content

You have amazing content ideas, and you want to share them with the world. But where do you start? How do you find the best place to showcase your talent and passion? The answer is simple: you need to choose the right platform to create your content.

- The right platform is the one that:

- Aligns with your content type and niche

- Connects you with a large and relevant audience

- Provides you with a user-friendly and secure interface

 - Rewards you with a low-cost and high commission

- Supports you with a good reputation and customer service

- Empowers you with good integration and customization options

To choose the right platform to create your content, you can:

- Compare the pros and cons of different platforms, such as your website, content platforms, or social media

- Consider the features and functionalities of different platforms, such as editing, hosting, analytics, etc.

- Consider the policies and regulations of different platforms, such as fees, taxes, refunds, disputes, etc.

- Consider the feedback and reviews of different platforms, such as customer satisfaction, creator support, etc.

- Consider the compatibility and flexibility of different platforms, such as design, branding, SEO, etc.

Some examples of platforms where you can create content online are:

- **Medium** is a platform where you can create and publish blog posts on various topics. You can also join publications, and fellow writers, and earn money from your content.

- **YouTube** is a platform where you can create and upload videos on various topics. You can also join channels, subscribe to creators, and earn money from your content.

- **Spotify** is a platform where you can create and distribute podcasts on various topics. You can also join shows, follow hosts, and earn money from your content.

- **Amazon Kindle** is a platform where you can create and sell ebooks on various topics. You can also join categories, follow authors, and earn money from your content.

- **Udemy** is a platform where you can create and sell courses on various topics. You can also join categories, follow instructors, and earn money from your content.

Section 3: Choosing the Right Monetization Methods for your Content

You have created awesome content, and you want to make money from it. But how do you do that?

How do you find the best way to monetize your content? The answer is simple: you need to choose the right monetization methods for your content.

The right monetization methods are the ones that

- Align with your content type and niche

- Align with your audience size and behavior

- Align with your revenue goals and expectations

- Comply with legal and tax requirements

- Ensure security and convenience

To choose the right monetization methods for your content, you can:

- Compare the pros and cons of different monetization methods, such as selling, advertising, sponsoring, etc.

- Consider the costs and benefits of different monetization methods, such as fees, commissions, discounts, etc.

- Consider the feedback and reviews of different monetization methods, such as customer satisfaction, creator support, etc.

- Consider the compatibility and flexibility of different monetization methods, such as integration, customization, etc.

- Consider the learning and improvement opportunities of different monetization methods, such as tutorials, courses, blogs, etc.

Some examples of monetization methods that you can use for your content online are:

- **Selling** is the method of charging a fee for your content, such as ebooks, courses, or memberships. You can sell your content on your website, or platforms like [Amazon Kindle] or [Udemy].

- **Advertising** is the method of displaying ads on your content, such as banners, pop-ups, or videos. You can display ads on your website, or platforms like Google Adsense or YouTube.

- **Sponsoring** is the method of partnering with brands or companies that pay you to promote their products or services on your content, such as reviews, shout-outs, or giveaways.

You can find sponsors on your own or on platforms like AspireIQ or [Podcorn]. This is a great way to leverage your influence and authority and earn money from your content. You can also provide value to your audience by introducing them to relevant and useful products or services that can solve their problems or enhance their lives.

- **Donating** is the method of asking your audience to support your content creation with voluntary contributions, such as tips, donations, or patronage. You can ask for donations on your website, or on platforms like [PayPal] or [Patreon]. This is a great way to show your gratitude and appreciation and build a loyal and engaged community. You can also provide value to your audience by offering them exclusive content, rewards, or perks that can make them feel special and appreciated.

Section 4: Choosing the Right Marketing and Promotion Strategies for your Content

You have created awesome content, and you want to make it reach more people. But how do you do that? How do you find the best way to market and promote your content? The answer is simple: you need to choose the right marketing and promotion strategies for your content.

The right marketing and promotion strategies are the ones that:

- Increase your content awareness and visibility

- Increase your content traffic and conversions

- Increase your content loyalty and retention

- Increase your content referrals and word-of-mouth

- Increase your content sales and revenue

To choose the right marketing and promotion strategies for your content, you can:

- Do market segmentation and find out your target market and audience, such as demographics, psychographics, behavior, etc.

This will help you understand who your ideal customers are, what they want, and how they behave.

- Do market positioning and find out your unique selling proposition and competitive advantage, such as benefits, features, values, etc.

This will help you differentiate yourself from your competitors, and communicate your value proposition to your audience.

- Do marketing mix and find out the best combination of product, price, place, and promotion, such as quality, value, distribution, and communication. This will help you optimize your product or service, set the right price, choose the right distribution channels, and create the right promotional mix.

- Do marketing channels and find out the best platforms and mediums to reach your audience, such as website, email, social media, etc. This will help you select the most effective and efficient ways to deliver your message to your audience.

- Do marketing tactics and find out the best methods and techniques to engage your audience, such as content, SEO, ads, etc.

This will help you create and execute the most impactful and relevant marketing campaigns for your audience.

- Do marketing metrics and find out the best ways to measure and improve your marketing performance, such as traffic, conversions, retention, etc. This will help you track and analyze your marketing results, and make data-driven decisions to improve your marketing ROI.

Section 5: Marketing and Promotion Strategies

Marketing and promotion strategies that you can use for your content online

 - **Content marketing** is the strategy of creating and distributing valuable, relevant, and consistent content to attract and retain your audience, and drive them to take action.

You can use content to educate your prospects, showcase your expertise, build trust, and solve their problems.

Some examples of content marketing formats are blog posts, ebooks, white papers, case studies, webinars, podcasts, and videos.

To succeed in content marketing, you need to have a clear understanding of your target audience, their needs, and their pain points. You also need to create a content calendar, optimize your content for SEO, and measure your results.

- **Social media marketing** is the strategy of using social platforms like Facebook, Twitter, Instagram, LinkedIn, and Pinterest to connect with your audience, increase your brand awareness, and generate more leads and sales.

You can use social media to share your content, engage with your followers, run ads, and participate in relevant conversations.

Some examples of social media marketing tactics are creating a social media profile, posting regularly, using hashtags, joining groups, hosting live sessions, and collaborating with influencers.

To succeed in social media marketing, you need to have a consistent voice and tone, choose the right platforms for your audience, create a posting schedule, and analyze your performance.

- **Email marketing** is the strategy of using email to connect with your audience, grow your leads, and turn them into customers. You can use email to deliver your content, share your offers, provide customer service, and build loyalty.

Some examples of email marketing campaigns are newsletters, welcome emails, lead magnets, product launches, cart abandonment emails, and re-engagement emails.

To succeed in email marketing, you need to have a permission-based email list, craft catchy subject lines, write engaging copy, design attractive layouts, and test your emails. Email marketing is one of the most powerful and personal ways to communicate with your audience, and drive them to take action.

These are some of the most common and effective marketing and promotion strategies that you can use for your content online. However, there are many more options that you can explore, such as SEO, PPC, influencer marketing, affiliate marketing, and more.

The key is to find the best mix of strategies that suit your goals, budget, and industry. You have the potential to reach millions of people online and make a positive impact with your content. With the right mindset and strategy, you can achieve anything

Chapter 5

Teaching Online

Your gift is a valuable contribution to the world. You have skills, knowledge, or expertise that can help others learn and grow. You are passionate about teaching and creating positive change. You can turn your gift into a profitable online income stream by teaching online. Teaching online is one of the most rewarding and lucrative ways to make money online.

You can teach subjects such as languages, math, music, or anything else that you are qualified to teach. You can create your courses, join a platform, or work as a tutor. You can teach online on your website, on online course platforms, or online tutoring platforms.

The Benefits of Teaching Online

The benefits of teaching online are:

- You have the opportunity to share your passion and knowledge with others

- You can reach a large and global audience of learners

- You can set your schedule and pace

- You can make money passively from your courses

- You can improve your teaching skills and credentials

The Challenges of Teaching Online

The challenges of teaching online are:

- You have to design and develop engaging and effective courses

- You have to provide feedback and support to your learners

- You have to deal with technical and pedagogical issues

- You have to comply with legal and ethical standards

- You have to market and promote your courses effectively

How to Succeed in Teaching Online

To succeed in teaching online, you need to:

- Choose the right subjects to teach

- Choose the best online platform to share your knowledge

- Choose the right pricing and payment methods for your courses

- Choose the right marketing and promotion strategies for your courses

- Choose the right tools and resources to support your online teaching

Section 1: Choosing the Right Subjects to Teach

The first step in teaching online is to choose the right subjects to teach. The right subjects are the ones that:

- Match your skills, interests, and passions

- Align your offerings with your target market's needs and wants

- Have a clear learning outcome and value

- Have a suitable level of difficulty and complexity

- Have a sufficient amount of content and material

To choose the right subjects to teach, you can:

- Do a self-assessment and find out your strengths and weaknesses, what you enjoy teaching, and what you are good at teaching

- Do market research and find out what your potential learners want and need, and what they are willing and able to pay

- Do competitor analysis and find out what your competitors are teaching and how they are teaching it

- Do subject validation and test your subject idea with your potential learners

- Do subject planning and outline your subject structure, format, and style

Some examples of subjects that you can teach online are:

- **Languages** are subjects that teach the skills and knowledge of a specific language, such as English, Spanish, or Mandarin. You can teach languages online on platforms like Preply or Italki. Teaching languages online is a great way to share your culture and experience, and help others communicate and connect with the world.

- **Math** is a subject that teaches the concepts and applications of mathematics, such as algebra, calculus, or statistics. You can teach math online on platforms like [Wyzant] or [Chegg Tutors]. Teaching math online is a great way to share your logic and creativity, and help others solve problems and achieve their goals.

- **Music** is a subject that teaches the skills and knowledge of a specific musical instrument, genre, or theory, such as piano, guitar, or jazz. You can teach music online on platforms like [TakeLessons] or [Lessonface]. Teaching music online is a great way to share your passion and talent, and help others express themselves and enjoy life.

Section 2: Choosing the Right Platform to Teach Online

You have chosen the right subjects to teach, and you are ready to create your courses. But where do you host them? How do you reach your learners?

How do you manage your online teaching? The answer is simple: you need to choose the right platform to teach online.

The right platform is the one that:

- Aligns with your subject type and niche

- Connects you with a large and relevant audience of learners

- Provides you with a user-friendly and secure interface

- Rewards you with a low-cost and high-commission

- Supports you with a good reputation and customer service

- Empowers you with good integration and customization options

To choose the right platform to teach online, you can:

 - Compare the pros and cons of different platforms, such as your website, online course platforms, or online tutoring platforms

- Consider the features and functionalities of different platforms, such as course creation, enrollment, communication, assessment, etc.

- Consider the policies and regulations of different platforms, such as fees, taxes, refunds, disputes, etc.

- Consider the feedback and reviews of different platforms, such as customer satisfaction, teacher support, etc.

- Consider the compatibility and flexibility of different platforms, such as design, branding, SEO, etc.

Some examples of platforms where you can teach online are:

 - **Udemy** is an online course platform that allows you to create and sell courses on various topics. You can also access tools, resources, and community on Udemy. Udemy is a great platform to showcase your expertise, reach millions of learners, and earn passive income from your courses.

- **Preply** is an online tutoring platform that allows you to teach languages to students from around the world. You can also access booking, payment, and feedback systems on Preply. Preply is a great platform to share your culture and experience, set your schedule and price, and get paid for each lesson you teach.

- **Skillshare** is an online course platform that allows you to create and share classes on creative topics, such as design, photography, or writing. You can also access analytics, royalties, and support on Skillshare. Skillshare is a great platform to share your passion and talent, join a vibrant community of creators, and earn money every time a student watches your class.

Section 3: Choosing the Right Pricing and Payment Methods for your Courses

You have created your courses, and you are ready to sell them. But how do you price them? How do you get paid? How do you manage your finances?

The answer is simple: you need to choose the right pricing and payment methods for your courses.

The right pricing and payment methods are the ones that:

- Reflect on the value and quality of your courses

- Attract and retain your learners

- Cover your costs and expenses

- Generate your desired profit

- Comply with legal and tax requirements

- Ensure security and convenience

To choose the right pricing and payment methods for your courses, you can:

- Do market research and find out what your learners are willing and able to pay

- Do competitor analysis and find out what your competitors are charging and offering

- Do cost analysis and find out your fixed and variable costs, such as platform fees, tools, taxes, etc.

- Do a profit analysis and find out your break-even point, profit margin, and revenue goals

- Do pricing strategies and find out the best pricing model, such as free, paid, subscription, etc.

- Do payment options and find out the best payment methods, such as credit cards, PayPal, Stripe, etc.

- Do payment security and find out the best payment gateways, such as SSL, PCI, etc.

Some examples of pricing and payment methods that you can use for your courses are:

- **Free** is the method of offering your courses for free, either as a lead magnet, a sample, or a goodwill gesture. You can use free courses to build your email list, showcase your value, or generate word-of-mouth.

- **Paid** is the method of charging a one-time fee for your courses, either as a single course, a bundle, or a package. You can use paid courses to generate immediate revenue, create scarcity, or offer discounts.

- **Subscription** is the method of charging a recurring fee for your courses, either as a membership, a subscription, or a club. You can use subscription courses to generate recurring revenue, create loyalty, or offer exclusivity.

Section 4: Choosing the Right Marketing and Promotion Strategies for your Courses

You have created your courses, and you are proud of them. But how do you spread the word? How do you attract and retain your learners? What strategies can you use to grow your online teaching business?

The answer is simple: you need to choose the right marketing and promotion strategies for your courses.

The right marketing and promotion strategies are the ones that:

- Increase your course awareness and visibility

- Increase your course enrollment and completion

- Increase your course loyalty and retention

- Increase your course referrals and word-of-mouth

- Increase your course sales and revenue

To choose the right marketing and promotion strategies for your courses, you can:

- Do market segmentation and find out your target market and audience, such as demographics, psychographics, behavior, etc. This will help you understand who your ideal learners are, what they want, and how they behave.

- Do market positioning and find out your unique selling proposition and competitive advantage, such as benefits, features, values, etc. This will help you differentiate yourself from your competitors, and communicate your value proposition to your learners.

- Do marketing mix and find out the best combination of product, price, place, and promotion, such as quality, value, distribution, and communication. This will help you optimize your course offering, set the right price, choose the right distribution channels, and create the right promotional mix.

- Do marketing channels and find out the best platforms and mediums to reach your learners, such as website, email, social media, etc. This will help you select the most effective and efficient ways to deliver your message to your learners.

- Do marketing tactics and find out the best methods and techniques to engage your learners, such as content, SEO, ads, etc. This will help you create and execute the most impactful and relevant marketing campaigns for your learners.

- Do marketing metrics and find out the best ways to measure and improve your marketing performance, such as enrollment, completion, retention, etc. This will help you track and analyze your marketing results, and make data-driven decisions to improve your marketing ROI.

Some examples of marketing and promotion strategies that you can use for your courses online are:

- **Content marketing** is the strategy of creating and distributing valuable, relevant, and consistent content to attract and retain your learners, and drive them to take action. You can use content marketing to showcase your expertise, provide value, and build trust with your learners. You can create content such as blog posts, videos, podcasts, ebooks, etc. Content marketing is one of the most powerful and cost-effective ways to market your courses online, and generate organic traffic and leads.

- **SEO** is the strategy of optimizing your website and content for search engines and users.

You can use SEO to increase your organic traffic, ranking, and visibility on search engines. You can optimize your website and content for keywords, titles, descriptions, links, etc. SEO is one of the most essential and long-term ways to market your courses online and boost your authority and credibility.

- **Ads** are the strategy of paying for displaying your courses on various platforms and mediums. You can use ads to increase your paid traffic, conversions, and sales. You can create ads such as banners, pop-ups, videos, etc. Ads are one of the most direct and immediate ways to market your courses online and reach your target audience and goals.

Section 5: Choosing the Right Tools and Resources to Support your Online Teaching

You have chosen the right platform, pricing, and marketing for your online teaching. But how do you manage and improve your online teaching? How do you save time and money?

How do you learn new skills and grow your business? The answer is simple: you need to choose the right tools and resources to support your online teaching.

The right tools and resources are the ones that:

- Simplify and automate your online teaching operations

- Enhance and optimize your online teaching performance

- Save and reduce your online teaching costs

- Learn and improve your online teaching skills

- Increase the size and scope of your online teaching enterprise

To choose the right tools and resources to support your online teaching, you can:

- Compare the features and functionalities of different tools and resources, such as course creation, enrollment, communication, assessment, etc.

- Consider the costs and benefits of different tools and resources, such as fees, commissions, discounts, etc.

- Consider the feedback and reviews of different tools and resources, such as customer satisfaction, teacher support, etc.

- Consider the compatibility and flexibility of different tools and resources, such as integration, customization, etc.

- Consider the learning and improvement opportunities of different tools and resources, such as tutorials, courses, blogs, etc.

Some examples of tools and resources that can help you teach online are:

- **Zoom** is a tool that helps you conduct video calls, webinars, and online meetings with your learners. You can also share your screen, record your sessions, and chat with your participants.

Zoom is a tool that makes your online teaching more interactive, engaging, and convenient.

You can also use Zoom to host live Q&A sessions, workshops, or master classes with your learners.

Teachable is a tool that helps you create and sell your online courses on your website. You can also access tools, resources, and community on Teachable. Teachable is a tool that makes your online teaching more professional, profitable, and scalable.

You can also use Teachable to create landing pages, sales pages, quizzes, certificates, and more for your courses.

Canva is a tool that helps you create and design beautiful and branded graphics, images, and videos for your online teaching. You can also access templates, icons, fonts, and colors on Canva.

Canva is a tool that makes your online teaching more attractive, creative, and consistent. You can also use Canva to create logos, banners, thumbnails, slides, and more for your online teaching.

Chapter 6

Investing Online

Do you have money to spare, and you want to make it grow? Do you wish to master your financial future and accomplish your dreams? You can do that by investing online. Investing online is one of the most exciting and rewarding ways to make money online.

You can invest your money in various financial assets, such as stocks, real estate, or cryptocurrencies, and earn returns from price appreciation, dividends, or interest. You can invest online on your own, with a robo-advisor, or with a broker. You can invest online on various platforms, such as online brokers, trading apps, or peer-to-peer lending platforms.

The benefits of Investing Online

The benefits of investing online are:

- You can access a wide range of investment opportunities

- You can diversify your portfolio and reduce your risk

- You can benefit from compound interest and long-term growth

- You can take advantage of market fluctuations and opportunities

- You can learn and improve your financial literacy and skills

The challenges of Investing Online

The challenges of investing online are:

- You have to deal with market volatility and uncertainty

- You have to research and analyze your investments carefully

- You have to manage your emotions and discipline

- You have to pay fees and taxes on your investments

- You have to protect your funds and identity from fraud and hacking

How to Succeed in Investing Online

To succeed in investing online, you need to:

- Choose the right investments to invest in

- Choose the right platform to invest online

- Choose the right strategy and style to invest online

- Choose the right tools and resources to support your online investing

- Choose the right mindset and habits to invest online

Each of these steps will be discussed in further detail in the subsequent sections.

Section 1: Choosing the Right Investments

The first step in investing online is to choose the right investments to invest in. The best investments are those that:

- Align your objectives, risk appetite, and time frame

- Have a high potential return and low risk

- Have a strong fundamental and technical performance

- Make a positive difference for society and the environment

- Benefit society and the environment in a positive way

- Have a low-cost and high liquidity

To choose the right investments to invest in, you can:

- Do a self-assessment and find out your investment objectives, risk profile, and investment horizon. This will help you clarify what you want to achieve, how much you can afford to lose, and how long you can wait for your returns.

- Do market research and find out the current trends, opportunities, and risks in the financial markets. This will help you understand the market conditions, the demand and supply, and the potential rewards and pitfalls of your investments.

- Do investment analysis and find out the valuation, growth, profitability, and quality of your potential investments. This will help you evaluate the performance, potential, and risk of your investments, and compare them with other alternatives.

- Do investment diversification and find out the optimal allocation of your assets, such as stocks, bonds, commodities, etc. This will help you balance your portfolio, and reduce your exposure to any single asset or market.

- Do investment selection and find out the best investments to buy, hold, or sell. This will help you make informed and timely decisions, and maximize your returns.

Some examples of investments that you can invest in online are:

Stocks

Stocks represent ownership stakes in a company that is traded on a stock market. You can earn returns from stock price appreciation, dividends, or stock splits. You can invest in stocks online on platforms like E*TRADE or Robinhood. Investing in stocks online is a great way to participate in the growth and success of your favorite companies, and benefit from their innovation and profitability.

Real estate

Real estate is properties that generate income from rent, appreciation, or capital gains. You can invest in real estate online on platforms like [Fundrise] or [RealtyMogul]. Investing in real estate online is a great way to own and manage properties without the hassle and cost of physical ownership, and benefit from their stability and appreciation.

Cryptocurrencies

Cryptocurrencies are a form of digital money that runs on a distributed network.You can earn returns from price fluctuations, mining, or staking.

You can invest in cryptocurrencies online on platforms like [Coinbase] or [Binance]. Investing in cryptocurrencies online is a great way to explore and experiment with the new and emerging technologies and trends, and benefit from their volatility and potential.

Section 2: Choosing the Right Platform to Invest Online

The second step in investing online is to choose the right platform to invest online. The platform that works best for you is the one that:

- Aligns with your investment type and niche

- Connects you with a large and relevant market

- Provides you with a user-friendly and secure interface

- Rewards you with a low-cost and high-commission

- Supports you with a good reputation and customer service

- Empowers you with good integration and customization options

To choose the right platform to invest online, you can:

- Compare the pros and cons of different platforms, such as your website, online brokers, trading apps, or peer-to-peer lending platforms. This will help you find the best fit for your investment needs, preferences, and goals.

- Consider the features and functionalities of different platforms, such as investment options, tools, resources, etc. This will help you find the best platform for your investment operations, performance, and improvement.

- Consider the policies and regulations of different platforms, such as fees, taxes, refunds, disputes, etc. This will help you find the best platform for your investment security, convenience, and compliance.

- Consider the feedback and reviews of different platforms, such as customer satisfaction, platform reliability, etc. This will help you find the best platform for your investment trust, confidence, and support.

- Consider the compatibility and flexibility of different platforms, such as integration, customization, etc. This will help you find the best platform for your investment design, branding, and optimization.

Some examples of platforms where you can invest online are:

E*TRADE

E*TRADE is an online broker that allows you to invest in stocks, bonds, ETFs, mutual funds, options, futures, and more. You can also access tools, resources, and education on E*TRADE. E*TRADE is a platform that makes your online investing easy, fast, and affordable. You can also enjoy low commissions, free trades, and no account minimums on ETRADE.

Fundrise

Fundrise is an online platform that allows you to invest in real estate projects across the US. You can also access tools, resources, and community on Fundrise. Fundrise is a platform that makes your online real estate investing accessible, diversified, and transparent. You can also enjoy low fees, high returns, and quarterly dividends on Fundraise.

Coinbase

Coinbase is an online platform that allows you to buy, sell, and store cryptocurrencies, such as Bitcoin, Ethereum, and Litecoin. You can also access tools, resources, and education on Coinbase. Coinbase is a platform that makes your online cryptocurrency investing simple, secure, and convenient. You can also enjoy low fees, high security, and instant transactions on Coinbase.

Section 3: Choosing the right strategy and style to invest online

You have chosen the right investments and the right platform to invest online. But how do you decide when and how to buy and sell them? How do you optimize your returns and minimize your risks? The answer is simple: you need to choose the right strategy and style to invest online.

The right strategy and style are the ones that:

-Align with your objectives, risk appetite, and duration

- Match your skills, knowledge, and experience

- Match your personality, temperament, and preferences

- Match your resources, tools, and platforms

- Match your market conditions, opportunities, and risks

To choose the right strategy and style to invest online, you can:

- Do a self-assessment and find out your investment profile, such as your objectives, risk appetite, and investment horizon. This will help you define what you want to achieve, how much you can afford to lose, and how long you can wait for your returns.

- Do strategy research and find out the different types of investment strategies, such as value, growth, income, etc. This will help you understand the different ways to invest, and the pros and cons of each strategy.

- Do style analysis and find out the different types of investment styles, such as active, passive, aggressive, conservative, etc. This will help you understand the different approaches to investing, and the advantages and disadvantages of each style.

- Do strategy selection and find out the best strategy and style for you, based on your investment profile, strategy research, and style analysis. This will help you choose the most suitable and effective way to invest, and the most compatible and comfortable way to invest.

- Do strategy execution follow your chosen strategy and style, and stick to your plan, rules, and discipline. This will help you implement your investment decisions, and achieve your investment goals.

Some examples of strategies and styles that you can use to invest online are:

Value investing

Value investing is a strategy that involves buying undervalued stocks that trade below their intrinsic value, and holding them until they reach their fair value. Value investing is a style that requires patience, research, and analysis. Value investing is suitable for investors who seek long-term growth, low risk, and high returns.

Growth investing

Growth investing is a strategy that involves buying high-growth stocks that have strong earnings, sales, and cash flow growth, and holding them until they reach their peak. Growth investing is a style that requires vision, innovation, and optimism. Growth investing is suitable for investors who seek short-term growth, high risk, and high returns.

Income investing

Income investing is a strategy that involves buying income-generating assets that pay regular dividends, interest, or rent, and holding them for a steady income stream. Income investing is a style that requires stability, consistency, and reliability. Income investing is suitable for investors who seek regular income, low risk, and moderate returns.

Choosing the right strategy and style to invest online can help you make the most of your online investing journey, and achieve your financial dreams.

Section 4: Choosing the Right Tools and Resources to Support your Online Investing

You have chosen the right investments, the right platform, and the right strategy and style to invest online. But how do you make your online investing easier, faster, and better? How do you save time and money? How do you learn new skills and grow your business? The answer is simple: you need to choose the right tools and resources to support your online investing.

The right tools and resources are the ones that:

- Simplify and automate your online investing operations

- Enhance and optimize your online investing performance

- Save and reduce your online investing costs

- Learn and improve your online investing skills

- Grow and scale your online investing business

To choose the right tools and resources to support your online investing, you can:

- Compare the features and functionalities of different tools and resources, such as trading, research, analysis, education, etc. This will help you find the best tools and resources for your online investing needs, preferences, and goals.

- Consider the costs and benefits of different tools and resources, such as fees, commissions, discounts, etc. This will help you find the best tools and resources for your online investing budget, profit, and ROI.

- Consider the feedback and reviews of different tools and resources, such as customer satisfaction, investor support, etc.

This will help you find the best tools and resources for your online investing trust, confidence, and support.

- Consider the compatibility and flexibility of different tools and resources, such as integration, customization, etc. This will help you find the best tools and resources for your online investing design, branding, and optimization.

- Consider the learning and improvement opportunities of different tools and resources, such as tutorials, courses, blogs, etc. This will help you find the best tools and resources for your online investing learning, improvement, and growth.

Some examples of tools and resources that can help you invest online are:

TradingView

TradingView is a tool that helps you analyze and trade various financial markets, such as stocks, forex, commodities, or cryptocurrencies. You can also access charts, indicators, signals, and community on TradingView. TradingView is a tool that makes your online investing more insightful, efficient, and profitable. You can also use TradingView to explore and test your trading ideas, strategies, and systems.

Yahoo! Finance

Yahoo! Finance is a tool that helps you research and monitor various financial markets, such as stocks, ETFs, bonds, or currencies. You can also access news, data, reports, and portfolios on Yahoo! Finance. Yahoo! Finance is a tool that makes your online investing more informed, updated, and organized. You can also use Yahoo! Finance to track and manage your investments, performance, and goals.

Investopedia

Investopedia is a tool that helps you learn and improve your financial literacy and skills, such as investing, trading, economics, or personal finance. You can also access articles, videos, courses, and simulators on Investopedia. Investopedia is a tool that makes your online investing more knowledgeable, skilled, and confident. You can also use Investopedia to learn and master the fundamentals, concepts, and techniques of online investing.

Section 5: Choosing the Right Mindset and Habits to Invest Online

You have everything you need to start and succeed in your online investing journey. But how do you stay focused, motivated, and disciplined? How do you deal with the ups and downs of the market? How do you keep learning and improving? The answer is simple: you need to choose the right mindset and habits to invest online.

The right mindset and habits are the ones that:

- Match your desired outcomes, risk comfort, and duration

- Align with your skills, knowledge, and experience

- Align with your personality, preferences, and emotions

- Align with your resources, tools, and systems

- Align with your performance, results, and feedback

To choose the right mindset and habits to invest online, you can:

- Develop the mindset and habits of successful investors, such as discipline, patience, confidence, curiosity, and humility.

This will help you follow your plan, rules, and discipline, and achieve your goals. This will also help you cope with the market volatility, uncertainty, and stress, and maintain your emotional balance.

- Avoid the mindset and habits of unsuccessful investors, such as greed, fear, overconfidence, bias, and regret. This will help you avoid making irrational, impulsive, and emotional decisions, and losing your money. This will also help you avoid missing out on opportunities, making mistakes, and blaming yourself or others.

Choosing the right mindset and habits to invest online can help you enjoy and excel in your online investing journey, and achieve your financial dreams.

Chapter 7

How to Scale and Diversify your Online Income Streams

You have a vision, a passion, and a skill. You have created your online income streams, and you are making money online. But you want more. You want to grow your revenue, reduce your risk, and explore new opportunities for your business. You can do that by scaling and diversifying your online income streams.

Scaling and diversifying your online income streams is a smart way to take your online business to the next level. You can create more value for your customers or clients, reach more people, and make more money.

You can also reduce your dependence on any single income stream, and protect yourself from any market changes or challenges. You can also discover new niches, trends, and possibilities for your online business.

Here are some steps you can take to scale and diversify your online income streams:

• **Identify your core competencies and skills.** What are you good at? What value can you offer to your customers or clients?

What are your unique selling points? These are the foundations of your online income streams.

You need to know your strengths and leverage them to create more products or services that solve problems or meet the needs of your target audience.

• **Research the market and the demand.** What are the problems or needs that your target audience has? How can you solve them or meet them with your products or services? What are the existing solutions or alternatives?

What are your unique selling points compared to the competitors? You need to know your market and your customers or clients and find the gaps and opportunities that you can fill or exploit with your products or services.

• Create multiple products or services based on your core competencies and skills. You can diversify your income by offering different types of products or services, such as physical products, digital products, courses, memberships, subscriptions, consulting, coaching, etc.

You can also diversify by offering different price points, packages, or tiers for your products or services. You need to create more value and options for your customers or clients and increase your income potential and sources.

• **Build an online presence and a brand.** You need to establish yourself as an authority and a trusted source in your niche. You can do this by creating a website, a blog, a podcast, a YouTube channel, a social media account, an email list, or any other platform that suits your audience and your goals.

You can also leverage existing platforms, such as Udemy, Skillshare, Amazon, Etsy, Fiverr, etc. to sell your products or services. You need to build your online reputation and credibility and attract and retain your customers or clients.

• **Promote and market your products or services**. You need to attract and retain customers or clients for your online income streams. You can do this by creating valuable and engaging content, offering freebies or discounts, running ads or campaigns, collaborating with influencers or partners, getting testimonials or reviews, etc.

You can also use SEO, email marketing, social media marketing, content marketing, or any other strategy that works for your niche and your audience. You need to spread the word and generate traffic, leads, and sales for your products or services.

• **Track and measure your results**. You need to monitor and analyze your online income streams to see what is working and what is not. You can use tools like Google Analytics, Facebook Pixel, or any other analytics software to track your traffic, conversions, sales, revenue, expenses, etc.

You can also use surveys, feedback forms, or polls to get insights from your customers or clients. You can then use this data to optimize and improve your products or services, your marketing, and your customer experience. You need to measure your performance and progress and make data-driven decisions to improve your online business.

• **Scale and diversify further.** You can scale and diversify your online income streams by creating more products or services, expanding to new markets or niches, adding new features or benefits, increasing your prices or margins, outsourcing or automating some tasks, etc.

You can also explore new opportunities or trends, such as affiliate marketing, dropshipping, podcasting, etc. The key is to keep learning, testing, and adapting to the changing needs and preferences of your audience and the market. You need to grow and scale your online business and achieve your online income goals.

Scaling and diversifying your online income streams is a smart way to increase your revenue, reduce your risk, and explore new opportunities for your business. It is also a fun and rewarding way to make money online and enjoy the freedom and flexibility of your online lifestyle.

So, what are you waiting for? Start scaling and diversifying your online income streams today, and make your online business a success.

How to Overcome the Common Obstacles and Challenges of Making Money online?

Making money online is a dream for many people, but it also comes with its own set of challenges and obstacles. You may feel overwhelmed, frustrated, or discouraged by the difficulties and risks of running an online business. But don't give up.

You can overcome any challenge and obstacle with the right mindset, attitude, and action. Here are some of the common ones and how to overcome them:

• **Lack of knowledge and skills**: If you want to succeed in any online business, you need to have the relevant knowledge and skills to provide value to your customers or clients. You can overcome this challenge by investing in your education and learning from experts, courses, books, blogs, podcasts, etc. You can also practice your skills by creating projects, portfolios, or samples of your work. You can turn your lack of knowledge and skills into an opportunity to learn, grow, and improve yourself and your online business.

• **Lack of patience and persistence:** Online businesses are not get-rich-quick schemes. They require time, effort, and dedication to grow and generate income. You can overcome this challenge by setting realistic goals and expectations, tracking your progress and results, celebrating your wins, and learning from your failures.

You can also find a mentor, a coach, or a community to support you and keep you motivated. You can turn your lack of patience and persistence into an opportunity to persevere, overcome, and achieve your online income goals.

• **Lack of preparedness and flexibility:** Online businesses are constantly evolving and changing due to market trends, customer preferences, technology updates, and competition. You can overcome this challenge by being prepared and flexible to adapt to the changes and opportunities.

You can do this by researching your niche and audience, testing your ideas and products, collecting feedback and data, and improving your offers and strategies. You can turn your lack of preparedness and flexibility into an opportunity to innovate, experiment, and optimize your online business.

• **Lack of data security and trust:** Online businesses are vulnerable to cyber-attacks, fraud, and scams that can harm your reputation and revenue. You can overcome this challenge by ensuring your data security and trust with your customers or clients.

You can do this by using reliable and secure platforms, tools, and software, updating your systems and passwords, encrypting your data and transactions, and complying with the relevant laws and regulations.

You can turn your lack of data security and trust into an opportunity to protect, reassure, and satisfy your customers or clients.

• **Lack of customer loyalty and retention:** Online businesses face a lot of competition and noise from other sellers and marketers. You can overcome this challenge by building customer loyalty and retention with your customers or clients. You can do this by creating and delivering high-quality products or services, providing excellent customer service and support, offering incentives and rewards, creating a brand and a community, and following up and engaging with your customers or clients.

You can turn your lack of customer loyalty and retention into an opportunity to attract, retain, and delight your customers or clients.

• **Lack of SEO and marketing skills:** Online businesses rely on SEO and marketing to attract and convert traffic into sales. You can overcome this challenge by improving your SEO and marketing skills and strategies.

You can do this by optimizing your website, blog, or store for search engines, keywords, and user experience, creating and distributing valuable and engaging content, using social media, email, and other channels to promote your offers and build relationships, and using analytics and tools to measure and optimize your performance and results.

You can turn your lack of SEO and marketing skills into an opportunity to learn, apply, and master the best practices and techniques of online marketing.

• **Lack of fulfillment and returns management:** Online businesses involve fulfilling and shipping orders, handling returns and refunds, and managing inventory and logistics. You can overcome this challenge by outsourcing or automating your fulfillment and returns management. You can do this by using a third-party fulfillment service, such as Red Stag Fulfillment, that can handle your orders, shipping, returns, and inventory for you, or using a dropshipping model, where you sell products from other suppliers and they handle the fulfillment and returns for you. You can turn your lack of fulfillment and returns management into an opportunity to save time, money, and hassle, and focus on your core competencies and skills.

Overcoming the common obstacles and challenges of making money online is not easy, but it is possible and rewarding. You can turn any challenge and obstacle into an opportunity to learn, grow, and improve yourself and your online business.

You can also use the right tools and resources to support your online income streams, and the right mindset and habits to invest online.

You can achieve anything you set your mind to, and make your online income dreams come true.

How to Stay Motivated and Inspired in your Online Income journey

You have a dream, a passion, and a skill. You have started your online income journey, and you are making money online. But you want more. You want to keep going, keep growing, and keep achieving. You can do that by staying motivated and inspired in your online income journey.

Motivation and inspiration are the fuel that drives your online income journey. They help you overcome the challenges and obstacles, and enjoy the rewards and opportunities. They help you stay focused, determined, and disciplined, and achieve your goals and dreams.

Here are some tips on how to stay motivated and inspired in your online income journey:

• **Remember your why:** Why did you start your online business in the first place? What is your vision, mission, and purpose? What are you passionate about? What impact do you want to make?

These are the questions that can help you reconnect with your why and remind you of the bigger picture. Your why is your source of intrinsic motivation and inspiration, and it can help you overcome any difficulties or doubts along the way.

• **Set SMART goals:** SMART stands for Specific, Measurable, Achievable, Relevant, and Time-bound. Setting SMART goals can help you stay motivated and inspired by giving you a clear direction, a way to track your progress, and a sense of accomplishment.

SMART goals also help you break down your big vision into smaller, manageable steps that you can focus on and achieve.

• **Celebrate your wins:** Celebrating your wins, no matter how big or small, can boost your motivation and inspiration by reinforcing your confidence, gratitude, and happiness. Celebrating your wins can also help you appreciate how far you've come, acknowledge your efforts and achievements, and reward yourself for your hard work. You can celebrate your wins by sharing them with others, treating yourself, or simply acknowledging them in your journal or planner.

• **Learn from your failures:** Failures are inevitable in any online income journey, but they are not the end of the world. Setbacks are occasions to gain insight, expand abilities, and boost results. Instead of letting failures discourage or demotivate you, use them as feedback and inspiration to do better next time.

You can learn from your failures by analyzing what went wrong, what you can do differently, and what you can do better.

• **Seek inspiration from others:** Sometimes, you may need some external sources of motivation and inspiration to keep you going. You can seek inspiration from others who have succeeded in their online income journey, such as mentors, role models, or peers.

You can learn from their stories, insights, and advice, and apply them to your situation. You can also seek inspiration from other sources, such as books, podcasts, blogs, videos, or quotes that resonate with you and your goals.

• **Surround yourself with positive people:** The people you surround yourself with can have a significant impact on your motivation and inspiration. Surround yourself with positive people who support, encourage, and inspire you, such as friends, family, or like-minded entrepreneurs.

Avoid negative people who drain, criticize, or discourage you, such as haters, naysayers, or complainers. Positive people can help you stay motivated and inspired by providing you with feedback, advice, or accountability.

• **Take care of yourself:** Taking care of yourself is crucial for maintaining your motivation and inspiration in your online income journey.

Taking care of yourself means taking care of your physical, mental, and emotional well-being, and ensuring that you have a healthy balance between your work and your life.

Taking care of yourself can help you stay motivated and inspired by preventing burnout, stress, or fatigue, and enhancing your energy, focus, and creativity.

You can take care of yourself by having a regular sleep schedule, eating well, exercising, meditating, relaxing, or doing something you enjoy.

Staying motivated and inspired in your online income journey is not easy, but it is possible and rewarding. You can use these tips to keep your motivation and inspiration high and keep your online income journey fun and exciting.

You can also use the right tools and resources to support your online income streams, and the right mindset and habits to invest online. You can achieve anything you set your mind to, and make your online income dreams come true.

Conclusion

You have reached the end of this book, but not the end of your online income journey. In this book, you have discovered how to make money online by exploring five different online income streams: selling products, selling services, creating content, teaching online, and investing online.

You have learned how to choose the right products, services, content, courses, and investments to sell online. You have learned how to choose the right platforms, pricing, monetization, marketing, and tools to support your online business. You have also learned the benefits and challenges of each online income stream and the best practices and tips to succeed in them.

By now, you should have a clear idea of what online income stream suits you best, and how to get started and grow your online income. You should also have a realistic and practical mindset that will help you overcome any obstacles and challenges that you may face along the way.

You should also have a vision and a plan that will guide you toward your online income goals and dreams.

But this is just the beginning. Some new trends and opportunities emerge every day. There are new skills and strategies that you can acquire and improve. There are new challenges and problems that you can solve and overcome.

That is why I encourage you to keep learning, experimenting, and improving your online income skills and knowledge. I also encourage you to join and connect with other online income enthusiasts and experts who can inspire and support you. I also encourage you to share and teach others what you have learned and experienced in your online income journey.

You have also learned how to overcome the common obstacles and challenges of making money online, how to stay motivated and inspired in your online income journey, and how to scale and diversify your online income streams.

But this book is not meant to be a definitive guide or a one-size-fits-all solution. It is meant to be a starting point, a catalyst, and a companion for your online income journey. It is meant to inspire you, inform you, and empower you to take action and achieve your online income goals.

The online world never stays the same, and neither should you. You should always be learning, testing, and adapting to the new realities and possibilities of the online market.

You should always be looking for new ways to create value, solve problems, and serve your customers or clients. You should always be striving for excellence, innovation, and growth.

Earning money online is challenging, but it is feasible and gratifying. You have the potential, the passion, and the skill to make money online. You have the vision, the mission, and the purpose to make money online.

You have the tools, the resources, and the systems to make money online.

You only need to take steps and make it a reality. So, what are you waiting for? Now, go and make some digital dollars online!